Let the Stones Cry Out

John Dillon

WESTBOW
PRESS®
A DIVISION OF THOMAS NELSON
& ZONDERVAN

WestBow Press books may be ordered through booksellers or by contacting:

WestBow Press
A Division of Thomas Nelson & Zondervan
1663 Liberty Drive
Bloomington, IN 47403
www.westbowpress.com
844-714-3454

ISBN: 978-1-6642-7848-6 (sc)
ISBN: 978-1-6642-7849-3 (e)

Library of Congress Control Number: 2022917153

Print information available on the last page.

WestBow Press rev. date: 11/8/2022

Introduction

God has blessed Nancie and me with wonderful travels this year. His creation is so beautiful! It is intricate, delicate, magnificent, colorful, majestic, surprising, peaceful, powerful, awe-inspiring, and so much more. All of creation is meant to point us to the Creator God, who loves us. He loves us so much that he gave his only Son to die on a cross. Jesus willingly accepted God's punishment for our sin so that we, through faith, might have forgiveness of sin and eternal life with him. During Jesus's triumphal entry into Jerusalem the crowds shouted, "Blessed is the King who comes in the name of the Lord! Peace in heaven and glory in the highest!"(Luke 19:38). But the religious leaders could not handle the people honoring Jesus, and so they asked Jesus to correct them. Jesus replied, "'I tell you, if these were silent, the very stones would cry out'" (Luke 19:40). On the following pages, I plan to share some of the many photos taken this year along with a scripture and/or Biblical principle that speaks to me through God's incredible creation. Let the stones cry out of God's creativity and love, and may we respond in humble worship.

This photograph is of an isolated shower outside of Montrose, Colorado. The West can often be seen as a dry and weary land. However, this photograph reminds me that there shall be showers of blessing even in the desert, and the greatest of these blessings is Jesus Christ.

Last January, we had a waterfront campsite in the Florida Keys. We were blessed with a number of spectacular sunrises. It was so peaceful. I am reminded of the following words in the praise song sung by Moses Hogan (written by Fernando Ortega): "In the morning when I rise give me Jesus / You can have all this world, but give me Jesus."[1]

---

[1] Fernando Ortega, "Give Me Jesus," Divine Hymns, accessed August 29, 2022, https://divinehymns.com/lyrics/give-me-jesus-fernando-ortega-song-lyrics/.

In the Everglades, we had the cool experience of seeing a flock of birds take off from a nearby pond. "Mountains and all hills, fruit trees and all cedars! Beasts and all livestock, creeping things and flying birds!…Let them praise the name of the Lord for his name alone is exalted; his majesty is above earth and heaven" (Psalm 148:9–10, 13). All creation points to God's beauty and majesty.

These photos are of ospreys in the Everglades. Notice the one bird has dinner in its talons. "'Look at the birds of the air: they neither sow nor reap nor gather into barns, and yet your heavenly Father feeds them. Are you not of more value than they?...But seek first the kingdom of God and his righteousness and all these things will be added to you'" (Matthew 6:26, 33).

More Everglades birds. The small bird is a purple gallinule. Its color is amazing and another example of God's beauty in creation. As stated in Genesis 1:20–21, "God said, 'Let birds fly above the earth across the expanse of the heavens.' So God created...every winged bird according to its kind. And God saw that it was good.'"

Having a bad hair day? This guy seems to know something is not quite right. "Humble yourselves, therefore, under the mighty hand of God so that at the proper time he may exalt you, casting all your anxieties on him, because he cares for you" (1 Peter 5:6–7). God may not remove our difficult situations, but he promises to walk with us through life's turmoil and bad hair days.

More Everglades birds. The bird on the right is a roseate spoonbill (top picture). It has a funny-looking bill, but its rose and pink feathers are really beautiful, even elegant (bottom picture). God doesn't make mistakes in his creation. We may look odd in the world's eyes, but *every* person has great value. A person whose heart honors God is always beautiful regardless of outward appearance.

These photographs were taken at sunset from Mallory Square, Key West. As the sun prepares to disappear below the western horizon, I am reminded of the psalmist who said, "As far as the east is from the west, so far does he remove our transgressions from us" (Psalm 103:12). Through Jesus's sacrifice on the cross, this is possible for anyone through faith. Let us give thanks!

First Peter 5:8 says, "Be sober-minded; be alert. Your adversary the devil prowls around like a roaring lion, seeking someone to devour." Okay, we didn't see a roaring lion in Florida, but how about a sneaky alligator? Today's society doesn't want to consider sin anymore. This thinking is just a part of Satan's deceit as he comes to us with tempting thoughts that promise pleasure but lead to destruction. We need to flee from the devil and cling to Jesus.

Here are a few Florida beach pictures. We really enjoyed Lovers Key State Park and Fort De Soto. The latter was a favorite, as the entire island is operated as a park by Pinellas County (St. Petersburg) with no private businesses or buildings and several miles of wide beach. Matthew 13:1–2 says, "That same day Jesus went out of the house and sat beside the sea. And great crowds gathered about him, so that he got into a boat and sat down. And the whole crowd stood on the beach." At this point in Jesus's life on earth, the crowds couldn't get enough of him. Are we that eager to see Jesus? Are we that eager to hear his Word?

"Behold, I am doing a new thing; now it springs forth, do you not perceive it? I will make a way in the wilderness and rivers in the desert" (Isaiah 43:19). Last April, we traveled to the Southwest. It was dry and barren but beautiful. This picture was taken in the southeast corner of Big Bend National Park. The river is the Rio Grande, and the Chisos Mountains are in the background. The photo and the verse from Isaiah serve as a reminder that even though we are dead in our sin, Jesus has made a way to bring life to us through his death on the cross and resurrection.

Big Bend National Park has two spectacular canyons: Boquillas Canyon in the southeast and Saint Elena Canyon in the southwest part of the park. The Rio Grande flows through both, and each canyon wall is 1,500 feet high. In both canyons, the United States is on one side of the river and Mexico on the other. In the Bible, water often symbolizes life. Jesus referred to the life he offers as "living water." As the life-giving water flows through the deep canyons, Psalm 23:4 comes to mind: "Even though I walk through the valley of the shadow of death, I will fear no evil, for you are with me; your rod and your staff, they comfort me." For Christians, God may not remove the dark days, but his promise is even better, for he is always with us.

Nancie and I went on an amazing five-mile hike in White Sands National Monument in southern New Mexico. You see nothing but sand, dunes, and mountains in the distance. It was a unique hike in that the "trail" was marked by posts in the sand. Occasionally, you could see several posts in the distance, but often your eyes could only see the next post. God created us not to be independent and self-sufficient but to be dependent on him. We should plan and work hard. Most importantly, we are to keep our eyes on him and walk by faith, not by sight. Proverbs 27:1 says, "Do not boast about tomorrow, for you do not know what a day may bring." This may be a scary verse, but as Christians we can rest and be secure in the knowledge that our Savior holds the future in his hands.

Chiricahua National Monument, in the southeast corner of Arizona, is noted for its rock pinnacles, many standing several hundred feet tall. Some of these formations seem to be precariously positioned; however, none fell while we hiked among them. Thank goodness! In 1 Corinthians 16:13, Paul encourages followers of Jesus to "be watchful," "be strong," and to "stand firm in [their] faith." In Ephesians 6:11, he encourages Christians to "put on the whole armor of God, that you may be able to stand against the schemes of the devil." Let's keep our eyes focused on Jesus to avoid toppling over.

This photograph is a saguaro cactus in Catalina State Park, just north of Tucson. In my weird imagination, it seems like this cactus, with its arms, is inviting us to "come here." The psalmist, in chapter 34:8, beckons us to come "taste and see that the Lord is good! Blessed is the man who takes refuge in him!" At Christmas and throughout the year, let us come to the manger and see the Christ child, Immanuel, God with us. Let us see the baby Jesus, who willingly gave up his position in heaven to come to this earth. He came not just to perform miracles and upset the religious leaders of the day but, most importantly, to die on a cross for the sins of the world. In response, and in the words of John Francis Wade, "Oh come let us adore Him, / Christ the Lord!"[2]

[2] John Francis Wade, "O Come Let Us Adore Him," Hymnary.org, accessed August 29, 2022, https://hymnary.org/text/o_come_let_us_adore_him.

These photos are from Catalina State Park, just north of Tucson. Paul writes to the Philippians "that he who began a good work in you will bring it to completion at the day of Jesus Christ. It is my prayer that your love may abound more and more, with knowledge and all discernment, filled with the fruit of righteousness that comes through Jesus Christ, to the glory and praise of God" (1:6, 9, 11). Cacti live in harsh, dry climates. After surviving the heat of summer and the cold, dry winter, cacti produce beautiful flowers for a few weeks in the spring. Similarly, Christians live in a dry, thirsty land, but God is working to mold us and change us to produce fruit (or flowers) in his time.

Organ Pipe Cactus National Monument is south of Phoenix on the Mexican border. The varieties of cacti pictured include organ pipe, teddy bear cholla, saguaro, prickly pear, ocotillo, and barrel. Also pictured is a desert tree called palo verde (Nancie and I call it the Shrek tree). I thought the trunk of a saguaro would have some give or cushion to it, but it was as hard as bark on any tree. All these plants are truly unique in the way they survive in the hot, dry climate. Ultimately, they have life because of water. Similarly, there is no life without the Living Water who is Jesus Christ. In John 4:11, the Samaritan woman asks, "'Where do you get that living water?'" Jesus answers in verse 14, "'The water that I will give him will become in him a spring of water welling up to eternal life.'"

These photos are of Watson Lake outside of Prescott, Arizona. This lake is surrounded by unusual rock formations that are fairly smooth and rounded. It reminds me that I am full of rough edges in my life, but his grace is still working on me. Joel Hemphill penned the children's song "He's Still Working On Me."[3] Thank God for his patient mercy and grace!

[3] Joel Hemphill, "He's Still Working on Me," Lyrics.com, accessed August 29, 2022, https://www.lyrics.com/lyric/7586805/He's+Still+Working+on+Me.

The red rock of Sedona, Arizona is really pretty. The top photo on the left is on top of Doe Mountain (a butte). The bottom photo is taken from downtown Sedona looking across at Table Top Mountain. The photo on this page is of Cathedral Rock. Sedona is a center for New Age thinking. Paul writes to the Colossians and warns them, "See to it that no one takes you captive by philosophy and empty deceit, according to human tradition, according to the elemental spirits of the world, and not according to Christ" (Col 2:8).

The top picture on the facing page is of the Colorado River in northern Arizona, upstream from the Grand Canyon. The bottom picture is in the Grand Staircase–Escalante National Monument, and the pictures on this page are of Grosvenor Arch in the same national monument. Many southwestern scenes are of a dry, weary land. Today's world is not much different. Yet we can have confidence in the Lord. Lamentations 3:22–24 says, "The steadfast love of the Lord never ceases; his mercies never come to an end; they are new every morning; great is your faithfulness. 'The Lord is my portion,' says my soul, 'therefore I will hope in him.'" There is hope and strength to be found, even in a dry, weary land.

These are a few pictures from Kodachrome State Park in southern Utah. It is amazing how, in just a matter of a few miles, a dry, barren, rocky desert turns into great beauty. Isaiah 61:3 says, "to grant to those who mourn in Zion—to give them a beautiful headdress instead of ashes, the oil of gladness instead of mourning, the garment of praise instead of a faint spirit." Beauty for ashes—God's handiwork in nature and in those that seek him.

This photo was taken just off Highway 12 outside of Bryce Canyon National Park. God's creation is so colorful. We are not to worship the creation, but rather the beauty of the Creator. The psalmist writes, "One thing have I asked of the Lord, that will I seek after: that I may dwell in the house of the Lord all the days of my life, to gaze upon the beauty of the Lord" (Psalm 27:4).

These photos are at The Toadstools east of Kanab, Utah. The bottom photo on the facing page is a bizarre landscape where bands of smooth red rock are sandwiched around a layer of white, very rough, crevassed hills. In the other toadstool photos, if you didn't know better, you would think that a crane must have been used to place these huge boulders on top of supporting pillars. In 1 Corinthians 10:12, Paul encourages the church in Corinth, "Therefore, let anyone who thinks he stands take heed, lest he fall." How do we stand? By being overwhelmed by God's incredible love for us.

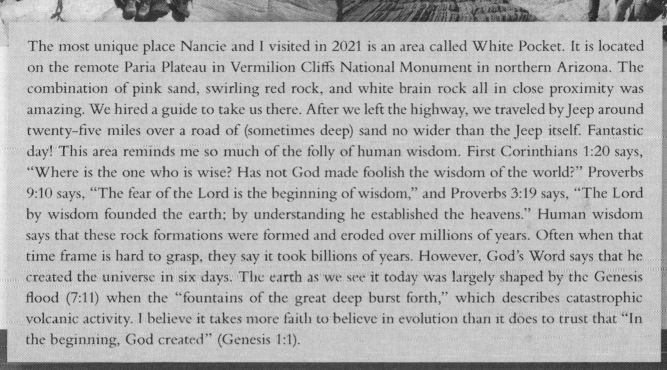

The most unique place Nancie and I visited in 2021 is an area called White Pocket. It is located on the remote Paria Plateau in Vermilion Cliffs National Monument in northern Arizona. The combination of pink sand, swirling red rock, and white brain rock all in close proximity was amazing. We hired a guide to take us there. After we left the highway, we traveled by Jeep around twenty-five miles over a road of (sometimes deep) sand no wider than the Jeep itself. Fantastic day! This area reminds me so much of the folly of human wisdom. First Corinthians 1:20 says, "Where is the one who is wise? Has not God made foolish the wisdom of the world?" Proverbs 9:10 says, "The fear of the Lord is the beginning of wisdom," and Proverbs 3:19 says, "The Lord by wisdom founded the earth; by understanding he established the heavens." Human wisdom says that these rock formations were formed and eroded over millions of years. Often when that time frame is hard to grasp, they say it took billions of years. However, God's Word says that he created the universe in six days. The earth as we see it today was largely shaped by the Genesis flood (7:11) when the "fountains of the great deep burst forth," which describes catastrophic volcanic activity. I believe it takes more faith to believe in evolution than it does to trust that "In the beginning, God created" (Genesis 1:1).

All aboard the Durango/Silverton (Colorado) narrow gauge railroad. Psalm 127:3 says, "Behold, children are a heritage from the Lord, the fruit of the womb a reward." I would add that grandchildren are a double blessing.

Winter tries hard to hold its grip in the high elevations of the Colorado Rockies. These photos were taken in the last week of April and first week of May. The photo in the upper left corner (facing page) is of Mt. Elbert, Colorado's highest peak. Most of the other locations are around the Lake Dillon area. The photo in the bottom right corner (facing page) is near Hoosier Pass looking at cloud-covered Mt. Quandary, just south of Breckenridge. The mountains await the promise of Spring. Psalms 30:5 says, "Weeping may tarry for the night, but joy comes with the morning." This life is filled with winters, and some of them may be long. However, in Christ, we can have a quiet confidence that he is in control and always with us. Springtime is coming. There will be joy in the morning.

A cold mountain stream is so refreshing! This is North Tenmile Creek outside of Frisco, Colorado. John writes in Revelation 7:17, "For the Lamb in the midst of the throne will be their shepherd, and he will guide them to springs of living water, and God will wipe away every tear from their eyes." Only the Lamb (Jesus) can provide what is ultimately satisfying. He wants to be our good Shepherd, to dwell with us, and to provide all that we truly need.

Grand Junction is located in a western Colorado valley. Dry arid mesas, plateaus, and mountains lie to its north and south. Were it not for the Colorado River flowing through the valley, it would be a wasteland. Just outside of the city rises Colorado National Monument, which contains towering monoliths, sheer cliffs, and red rock canyons. This national monument is a hidden gem. The landscape reminds me of the lyrics from an old hymn written by Fanny Crosby: "He hideth my soul in the cleft of the rock / that shadows a dry, thirsty land. He hideth my life in the depths of his love / and covers me there with his hand."[4] Salvation is a gift of God through faith in Jesus Christ. God continues to lavish his grace upon us with protection.

---

[4] Fanny Crosby, "He Hideth My Soul," Hymnal.net, accessed August 22, 2022, https://www.hymnal.net/en/hymn/h/334.

More photos from Colorado National Monument. Our campsite was about 100 yards from one of these cliffs. Driving through the park produced many a queasy feeling as the road wound treacherously close to the cliffs. Most of the time, there were no guardrails to protect from the nearby danger. Thank God that, for believers in Christ, none of life's situations, no matter how dangerous or difficult, can remove us from the love of God. Paul says in Romans 8:35, "Who shall separate us from the love of Christ? Shall tribulation, or distress, or persecution, or famine, or nakedness, or danger, or sword?" Rest in him!

Black Canyon of the Gunnison National Park is located in western Colorado. The steepest part of the canyon is almost ten miles long with depths ranging from 1,800 to 2,400 feet. The width of the canyon at one point is as narrow as 1,300 feet. The north rim is fairly remote, accessible by dirt road. These photographs were taken from the north side of the canyon except for the one below which shows a cliff face with striated rock and the Gunnison River flowing through this incredibly deep canyon. No matter how deep life's canyons have been, there is living water that can flow right through them. That living water is available through faith in Jesus's death and resurrection. No matter how messed up our lives have been, God's love and grace is greater. Point of Grace had a song titled "There Is Nothing Greater Than Grace" (written by Samuel Mizell, Marshall Hall, and Antonio Neal) that was released in 2010. In the chorus it says, "There is no heartbreak he can't take you through. / So before you think that you're too lost to save, / remember there is nothing greater than grace."[5]

[5] Antonio Neal, Marshall Hall, and Samuel C. Mizell, "There Is Nothing Greater Than Grace," AZLyrics.com, accessed August 29, 2022, https://www.azlyrics.com/lyrics/pointofgrace/thereisnothinggreaterthangrace.html.

As Nancie and I rode our tandem bicycle near the south rim of the Black Canyon of the Gunnison National Park near Montrose, Colorado, we saw this wonderful scene: a few isolated showers in the distance while the sun dipped behind the clouds. Even in the dry times of life, God provides. He doesn't promise to give us our wants, but he does promise to give us what we need. In our western culture, there has been incredible confusion between "wants" and "needs." Let us remember that everything we have is a gift from God. In John 3:27, John the Baptist says, "'A person cannot receive even one thing unless it is given him from heaven.'" Let us realize that our greatest need is Christ.

Nancie and I enjoyed a beautiful campsite in Ridgway State Park in western Colorado. The above photo is looking south to the San Juan Mountains. Both photos are at overlooks above Ridgway Reservoir. Second Peter 3:8–9 says, "But do not overlook this one fact, beloved, that with the Lord one day is as a thousand years, and a thousand years as one day. The Lord is not slow to fulfill his promise as some count slowness, but is patient toward you, not wishing that any should perish, but that all should reach repentance." God wants a relationship with everyone. He calls us to repent of our pride and self-centeredness and turn to him.

Telluride is a beautiful, small town nestled at the end of a valley in the San Juan Mountains of southwestern Colorado. Psalm 125:2 says, "As the mountains surround Jerusalem, so the Lord surrounds his people, from this time forth and forevermore." Although this world seems to be spinning out of control, the children of God can have confidence that his loving and strong arms will always surround us.

Just outside of Telluride are several hiking trails leading to beautiful waterfalls. The photo below is on Bear Creek Trail. The other trail goes by several unnamed falls to Bridal Veil Falls. It is amazing that southwestern Colorado has been in a severe drought for a number of years, but these falls never run dry. Let us be reminded that "Your love never fails, / it never gives up, / it never runs out on me."[6] This song was penned by Brian Johnson, Jeremy Riddle, and Christa Black Gifford. David writes in Psalm 52:1, and 8–9, "The steadfast love of God endures all the day. I trust in the steadfast love of God forever and ever. I will thank you forever, because you have done it. I will wait for your name, for it is good, in the presence of the godly." Although I don't deserve any of it, God pours out his love, and he never gives up. Lord, help me to fully trust in that love.

[6] Brian Johnson, Jeremy Riddle, and Christa Black Gifford, "One Thing Remains," Lyrics.com, accessed August 29, 2022, https://www.lyrics.com/lyric/22163090/Jesus+Culture/One+Thing+Remains.

Oh, the joys of family! The photos include the troops up at Independence Pass east of Aspen, Colorado; Erin and Griffin on top of a rock east of Aspen; our four adorable grandchildren at Windsor Lake outside Leadville, Colorado; and a family photo at Windsor Lake. Psalm 127:3 says, "Behold, children are a heritage from the Lord." Proverbs 17:6 says, "Grandchildren are the crown of the aged." Children are gifts from God, cherished and loved. Somehow, grandkids are even sweeter—the icing on the cake.

Windsor Lake is a short, but steep, hike outside of Leadville, Colorado. It is one of the prettiest alpine lakes I have experienced. The beauty of the mountains, the trees, and the crystal clear water is breathtaking and refreshing. God provides living water through Jesus Christ, yet many reject him and go their own way. Jeremiah 2:13 says, "For my people have committed two evils: they have forsaken me, the fountain of living waters, and hewed out cisterns for themselves, broken cisterns that can hold no water." Men's and women's pursuit of happiness in fame, profit, or pleasure ends up in hopelessness. Jesus says in John 14:6, "I am the way, the truth, and the life."

These pictures are of wonderful friends who joined us in colorful Colorado. Scenes include Loveland Pass, Rocky Mountain National Park, Berthoud Pass, Independence Pass, hiking near the Maroon Bells (Aspen), and the top of Mt. Evans. A road reaches within a quarter mile of the summit of Mt. Evans providing easy access to one of Colorado's Fourteeners. It is truly a unique experience being on top. Being with friends and sharing in God's creation is a wonderful experience. Much greater is when we go to his house (when we are in central Colorado, it's Agape Outpost in Breckenridge) and worship him together. Psalm 95:1, 2, 4, and 6 says,

Oh come, let us sing to the Lord; let us make a joyful noise to the rock of our salvation! Let us come into his presence with thanksgiving; let us make a joyful noise to him with songs of praise! In his hand are the depths of the earth; the heights of the mountains are his also. Oh come, let us worship and bow down; let us kneel before the Lord, our Maker!

The photos on the left page are at Guanella Pass. It is the trailhead for Mt. Bierstadt (bottom photo) which Nancie and I hiked several years ago. The photos on this page are from the top of Mt. Evans. Both mountains are Fourteeners in central Colorado. These bring to mind Psalm 90:2, 10, 12, and 14:

> Before the mountains were brought forth, or ever you had formed the earth and the world, from everlasting to everlasting you are God. The years of our life are seventy, or even by reason of strength eighty; so teach us to number our days that we may get a heart of wisdom. Satisfy us in the morning with your steadfast love.

God is the sovereign, almighty creator of the universe. We are but dust or grass in the wind. May he give us the wisdom to recognize our pride, turn from it, and then seek him wholeheartedly, letting his love be our only satisfaction.

These are scenes from Independence Pass, Colorado. Mountains point to the majestic power and beauty of God's creation. Psalm 96:6, 8, and 9 says, "Splendor and majesty are before him; strength and beauty are in his sanctuary. Ascribe to the Lord glory and strength! Worship the Lord in the splendor of holiness; tremble before him, all the earth!" This powerful God is sovereign over his creation. Yes, even in these crazy times, he is in control. This same God reveals his love in the intricate beauty displayed throughout creation. All of nature points to our majestic and beautiful God.

Thunderstorms are brewing over the Maroon Bells near Aspen, Colorado. As the clouds build, the flowers seem unfazed as they display their beauty. David prays to God as he runs for his life in Psalm 57:1, 7, and 10: "Be merciful to me, O God, be merciful to me for in you my soul takes refuge; in the shadow of your wings I will take refuge, till the storms of destruction pass by. My heart is steadfast, O God, my heart is steadfast! For your steadfast love is great to the heavens, your faithfulness to the clouds." Even when the storm clouds come, may we be confident in his shelter, and the victory we have in Jesus.

The Crooked River winds around unique rock formations in Smith Rock State Park in Oregon. The rock pillar (above right) is called Monkey Face. David, in Psalm 36:7–9, says, "How precious is your steadfast love, O God! The children of mankind take refuge in the shadow of your wings. They feast on the abundance of your house, and you give them drink from the river of your delights. For with you is the fountain of life; in your light do we see light." God has given us a river of delights and shown us true life in Jesus Christ. Why do we continually wander from the riverbank? If we really understood his steadfast love, we would build our homes on the river and never leave.

Steelhead Falls are on the Deschutes River near Terrebonne, Oregon. A short hike leads through a beautiful valley before reaching the falls. In Isaiah 43:1 and 2, God says to his people, "Fear not, for I have redeemed you; I have called you by name, you are mine. When you pass through the waters, I will be with you; and through the rivers, they shall not overwhelm you." As the children of God, we are eternally secure. We have been purchased with the precious blood of Jesus. People can harm the body, but the soul can rest on the solid rock.

My sister Sharon and husband Ed were able to join Nancie and me on our tour of Oregon. They live in the state of Washington, so we don't get to see them very often. It was truly wonderful to spend several weeks with them. Romans 10:15 says, "How beautiful are the feet of those who preach the good news." Ed and Sharon are a wonderful Christian couple whose goal is to point people to Jesus.

Mt. Hood dominates the landscape east of Portland, Oregon. Between its elevation (11,249 feet) and latitude, Mt. Hood is able to have a ski resort (south facing) that is open year-round. Part of the chorus of Robert Robinson's hymn "Come, Thou Fount of Every Blessing" is "Praise the mount I'm fixed upon it / mount of Thy redeeming love." Let the following words from this song be our prayer:

Come, Thou Fount of every blessing,
tune my heart to sing Thy grace;
streams of mercy, never ceasing,
call for songs of loudest praise.
Jesus sought me when a stranger,
Wand'ring from the fold of God;
He, to save my soul from danger,
interposed His precious blood…
Prone to wander, Lord, I feel it;
Prone to leave the God I love.
Take my heart, oh, take and seal it
With Thy Spirit from above.[7]

---

[7] Robert Robinson, "Come, Thou Fount of Every Blessing,"Hymnal.net, accessed August 29, 2022, https://www.hymnal.net/en/hymn/h/319#1.

An incredible gem in Oregon's State Park system lies east of Salem. Silver Falls State Park is home to the Trail of Ten Falls. Several of the falls exceed 170 feet in height and a hiker can walk behind four of the falls. A number of these photographs use a longer shutter exposure, which creates the smooth, blurred effect of the falling water. The naked eye certainly cannot see what the camera produces. In 2 Corinthians 4:18, Christians are encouraged to "look not to the things that are seen but to the things that are unseen." In verse 1 of chapter 11, the author of Hebrews says, "Now faith is the assurance of things hoped for, the conviction of things not seen." I have often thought that the unseen is more real than what we see. We can have absolute confidence that the Creator of the universe loves us because he gave his Son to die in our places, and he was victorious over the grave. Let's walk in that steadfast love.

The Oregon coast is simply spectacular! This photo is taken from Ecola State Park, which is just north of Cannon Beach (in the distance). Isaiah 48:18 says, "Oh that you had paid attention to my commandments! Then your peace would have been like a river, and your righteousness like the waves of the sea." The sin nature inside all of us tempts us to find satisfaction or fulfillment in everything but God. However, he alone offers and provides peace and life, now and eternally.

The Oregon coast has mile after mile of beautiful beaches with monoliths and other rock structures along the shoreline. This picture reminds me of the words from an old hymn written by Edward Mote: "My hope is built on nothing less than Jesus' blood and righteousness...On Christ the solid rock I stand, / all other ground is sinking sand."[8] There is only one firm foundation in this life.

---

[8] Edward Mote, "My Hope is Built on Nothing Less," Hymnary.org, accessed August 29, 2022, https://hymnary.org/text/my_hope_is_built_on_nothing_less.

These photos are from Ecola State Park and the Cannon Beach area along the northern coast of Oregon. Be in awe at God's creation! On a macro level, we see his beauty in the beach landscapes. However, in his wisdom, and on a micro level, he also created the intricate ecosystems where various forms of life are dependent on each other for survival. He is sovereign and holds it all together. Nehemiah 9:6 says, "You are the Lord, you alone. You have made heaven, the heaven of heavens, with all their host, the earth and all that is on it, the seas and all that is in them; and you preserve all of them."

The Heceta Head Lighthouse is located north of Florence and is one of eleven lighthouses on the Oregon coast. The psalmist in chapter 119, verses 105, 160, and 11 says, "Your word is a lamp to my feet and a light to my path. The sum of your word is truth, and every one of your righteous rules endures forever. I have stored up your word in my heart, that I might not sin against you." Unlike humans, whose rules constantly change, God's Word is the same yesterday, today, and tomorrow. Let us treasure the light and truth of his Word.

The beaches of Oregon are quite diverse. Many have rock formations beyond the surf. The photographs above and to the left are from the Oregon Dune National Recreation Area where the beach itself is filled with dunes. Deuteronomy 33:19 says, "They shall call peoples to their mountain; there they offer right sacrifices; for they draw from the abundance of the seas and the hidden treasures of the sand." The beauty of the seas and sand point us to a wonderful God. Let us seek to worship him rightly. David, in Psalm 51:17, describes how we should approach worship: "The sacrifices of God are a broken spirit; a broken and contrite heart, O God, you will not despise." Our sin has us in desperate need of a Savior, who is Jesus Christ. Oh what a wonderful, merciful Savior!

The Samuel Boardman State Scenic Corridor is a spectacular twelve-mile coastline north of Brookings in southwest Oregon. Highway 101 winds through this corridor around craggy cliffs and thick forests along the rugged coast. This ocean corridor also has a number of secluded sandy beaches including Secret Beach, which is featured in the pictures. "For the earth will be filled with the knowledge of the glory of the Lord as the waters cover the sea" (Habakkuk 2:14). God's mighty power and beauty is on display on the Oregon coast. One day, all the earth will know that this was his mighty hand in creation.

These photographs were taken late in the afternoon on Cape Ferrelo north of Brookings, Oregon. A short hike out to the cape's point provided incredible views looking both north and south, overlooking the end of the rugged coastline as it gives way to the Pacific Ocean. As the prophet Isaiah said,

> Have you not known? Have you not heard? The Lord is the everlasting God, the Creator of the ends of the earth. He does not faint or grow weary; his understanding is unsearchable. They who wait for the Lord shall renew their strength; they shall mount up with wings like eagles; they shall run and not be weary; they shall walk and not faint. (40:28 and 31)

The Creator of this beauty is beyond our comprehension, but if we seek him, he will provide peace and strength.

These awesome dudes (our grandsons Griffin and Everett) made it all the way to Timberline Lake! The Timberline Lake Trail is 5.5 miles and gains 900 feet to an elevation of 10,850 feet. Its conclusion is this peaceful, alpine lake west of Leadville, Colorado. Griffin hiked the entire way. Everett had just a bit of help from momma…or, okay, maybe a lot of help. Alpine lakes are so peaceful and refreshing. The psalmist cries to the Lord, "As a deer pants for flowing streams, so pants my soul for you, O God. My soul thirsts for God, for the living God" (42:1 and 2). We were created for a relationship with God. Only he can fill that longing in our lives.

Just west of Laramie, Wyoming is the Snowy Range Scenic Byway which crosses the Medicine Bow Mountain Range. This drive winds up into the mountains, where pristine lakes meet quartzite peaks. Nancie and I hiked up to Medicine Bow Peak, gaining 1,240 feet of elevation to the summit at 11,940 feet. Amos 4:13 says, "For behold, he who forms the mountains and creates the wind, and declares to man what is his thought, who makes the morning darkness, and treads on the heights of the earth— the Lord, the God of Hosts, is his name!" The Lord God, creator of the universe, has declared his thought through the Bible, and has declared his incredible love for us through his Son, Jesus Christ.

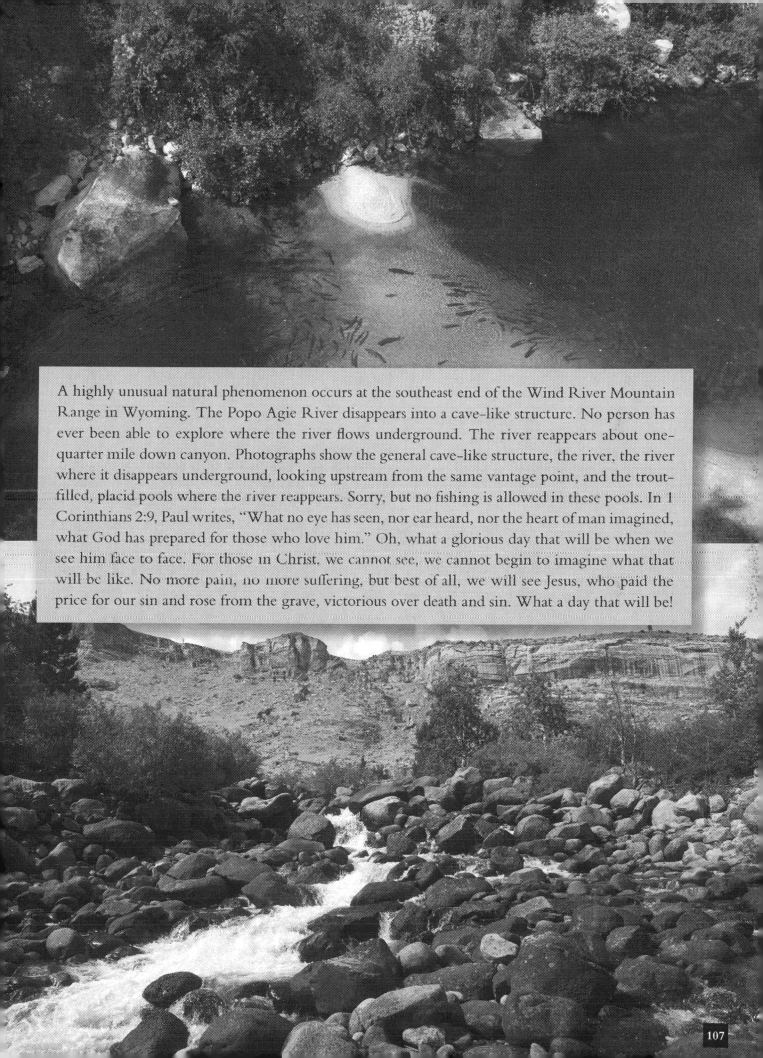

A highly unusual natural phenomenon occurs at the southeast end of the Wind River Mountain Range in Wyoming. The Popo Agie River disappears into a cave–like structure. No person has ever been able to explore where the river flows underground. The river reappears about one-quarter mile down canyon. Photographs show the general cave–like structure, the river, the river where it disappears underground, looking upstream from the same vantage point, and the trout-filled, placid pools where the river reappears. Sorry, but no fishing is allowed in these pools. In 1 Corinthians 2:9, Paul writes, "What no eye has seen, nor ear heard, nor the heart of man imagined, what God has prepared for those who love him." Oh, what a glorious day that will be when we see him face to face. For those in Christ, we cannot see, we cannot begin to imagine what that will be like. No more pain, no more suffering, but best of all, we will see Jesus, who paid the price for our sin and rose from the grave, victorious over death and sin. What a day that will be!

The Lower Falls of the Yellowstone River tumbles 308 feet into a canyon whose color gives the national park its name. From a distance at Artist's Point (view of photograph), the setting is serene. The experience dramatically changes, however, as one approaches the falls and hears and feels the water's roar. Revelation 19:6 says, "Then I heard what seemed to be the voice of a great multitude, like the roar of many waters, crying out, 'Hallelujah! For the Lord our God Almighty reigns.'" There is coming a day when God will call an end to this present age. At that time, there will be people in Christ from all races gathered together singing in one voice. This will be history's greatest worship experience.

As we traveled into Yellowstone National Park, we were greeted by this red fox. Foxes are primarily nocturnal animals, so this was a rare sighting. As recorded in Matthew 8:20, Jesus said, "'Foxes have holes, and birds of the air have nests, but the Son of Man has nowhere to lay his head.'" Jesus, the Son of God, gave up his position in heaven to walk this earth, live a perfect life, and then die a cruel and humiliating death. With his crucifixion, he paid the price for the sin of humankind. He left the treasures of heaven because of love—a love that was victorious over sin, death, and the grave, a love that is available to all people through faith.

Yellowstone National Park is best known for its geysers and other thermal features, but scenic rivers flow throughout the park. Some quietly make their way through peaceful valleys, while others tumble over cascades, and others plunge over falls. These rivers support an abundance of wildlife and greatly add to the beauty of the park. In Psalm 36:7–9, David says, "How precious is your steadfast love, O God! The children of mankind take refuge in the shadow of your wings. They feast on the abundance of your house, and you give them drink from the river of your delights. For with you is the fountain of life; in your light do we see light."

Yellowstone National Park's thermal features are magnificent. Beautiful colors and warm, crystal clear waters invite tourists to take a closer look. However, there are boardwalks constructed near these pools for safety. Warnings are posted: "Danger! Stay on the walkway." A person could easily fall through the earth's thin crust. Proverbs 14:12 says, "There is a way that seems right to a man, but its end is the way to death." Then the psalmist (119:37) writes, "Turn my eyes from looking at worthless things; and give me life in your ways." The ways of this world always seem attractive, but they bring destruction. There is real life to be found—in Jesus.

What is going to Yellowstone National Park without seeing Old Faithful geyser? This famous attraction erupts twenty times daily. True to its name, eruptions are predicted with a 90 percent confidence rate, within a ten-minute variation, based on the duration and height of the previous eruption. Eruptions last between 1.5 and 5 minutes, vary in height from 100 to 180 feet, and spew between 4,000 to 8,000 gallons of water into the air. There is One who is perfectly faithful. The words to a favorite hymn written by Thomas Chisholm are as follows: "Great is Thy faithfulness, O God my Father, / there is no shadow of turning with Thee. / Thou changest not, Thy compassions, they fail not; as Thou hast been, Thou forever wilt be."[9] He never changes. He is the same today as he was a thousand years ago, and he will be the same for eternity. May his faithfulness and love so overwhelm us that we see the new mercies he provides every morning.

[9] Thomas Chisolm, "Great Is Thy Faithfulness," Hymnary.org, accessed August 29, 2022, https://hymnary.org/text/great_is_thy_faithfulness_o_god_my_fathe.

Elk are beautiful animals, strong and majestic. They are the largest species within the deer family and are also known as wapiti. These photos were taken near Mammoth Hot Springs in the northwest corner of Yellowstone National Park. We read in Genesis 1:24 and 25 that "God said, 'Let the earth bring forth living creatures according to their kinds—livestock and creeping things and beasts of the earth according to their kinds.' And it was so. And God saw that it was good." God created all creatures according to their kinds. Yes, over time there have been small changes within species. However, the theory of evolution has so many holes that simply can't be explained, and change from one species to another is only one example. Evolution is a theory that is wobbly at best. Trust God's Word when it simply says that he spoke it into existence.

Wonderful friends joined us for our travels in Yellowstone and Teton National Parks. The author of Hebrews encourages Christians to "strive for peace with everyone" (12:14). This is especially true when I want to go on "killer" hikes and the four of us are in close quarters in the RV. Paul, writing to the Corinthians, says, "Blessed be the God and Father of our Lord Jesus Christ, the Father of mercies and God of all comfort, who comforts us in all our affliction, so that we may be able to comfort those who are in any affliction, with the comfort with which we ourselves are comforted by God" (2 Co. 1:3 and 4). In Romans 12:15, Paul encourages the body to "rejoice with those who rejoice, weep with those who weep." What a wonderful blessing is the body of Christ.

Yellowstone National Park is a land of many waters: beautiful lakes, amazing thermal features (geysers and springs), and rivers. These photographs are several of the waterfalls in the park. Traveling out west, one can easily see the importance of water. Without water, the land is parched with little life. However, wherever there is water, both plant and animal life thrive. In John 7:37 and 38, Jesus cries out, "'If anyone thirsts, let him come to me and drink. Whoever believes in me, as the Scripture has said, "Out of his heart will flow rivers of living water."'" Later, according to John 10:10, Jesus said, "'I came that they may have life and have it abundantly.'" God placed within humans a thirst for purpose and fulfillment. He is the sole source for true life, abundant life.

Similar to Yellowstone, its neighboring national park to the north, Grand Teton National Park is home to a great diversity of wildlife. A National Elk Refuge is north of the town of Jackson, where an average of 7,500 elk endure the harsh winter. The elk leave the refuge in spring, follow the melting snow line into the mountains, and then migrate back to the refuge in December. Moose frequent willow meadows and marshy areas, especially at dawn and dusk. Pronghorn are the fastest land animals in the western hemisphere, capable of running speeds of fifty-five miles per hour. They, along with bison, are common in the flats of the park. Amos 5:22 says, "Even though you offer me your burnt offerings and grain offerings, I will not accept them; and the peace offerings of your fattened animals, I will not look upon them." God does not want us to go through the motions. The prophet Amos tells us that religion can actually hinder our relationship with God. In 1 Samuel 15:22, Samuel says, "Has the Lord as great delight in burnt offerings and sacrifices, as in obeying the voice of the Lord? Behold, to obey is better than sacrifice." God wants our hearts, not our religious habits.

Jackson Hole is the valley lying between the Teton and Gros Ventre Mountain ranges in northwestern Wyoming. The valley is approximately forty-eight miles long with widths varying between eight and fifteen miles wide. The Teton Mountain range is perhaps the prettiest in the country. It is unique with its absence of foothills. Nestled against the mountains on the west side of the valley is a string of lakes. The mountains skyrocket to heights as much as 7,000 feet above the valley floor. We were so blessed to experience a spectacular sunset in the valley. Psalm 113:3 says, "From the rising of the sun to its setting, the name of the Lord is to be praised!" We were created to worship our mighty God, the creator of the universe. Our greatest goal in life should be to worship him and to know him with his incredible beauty and love for us.

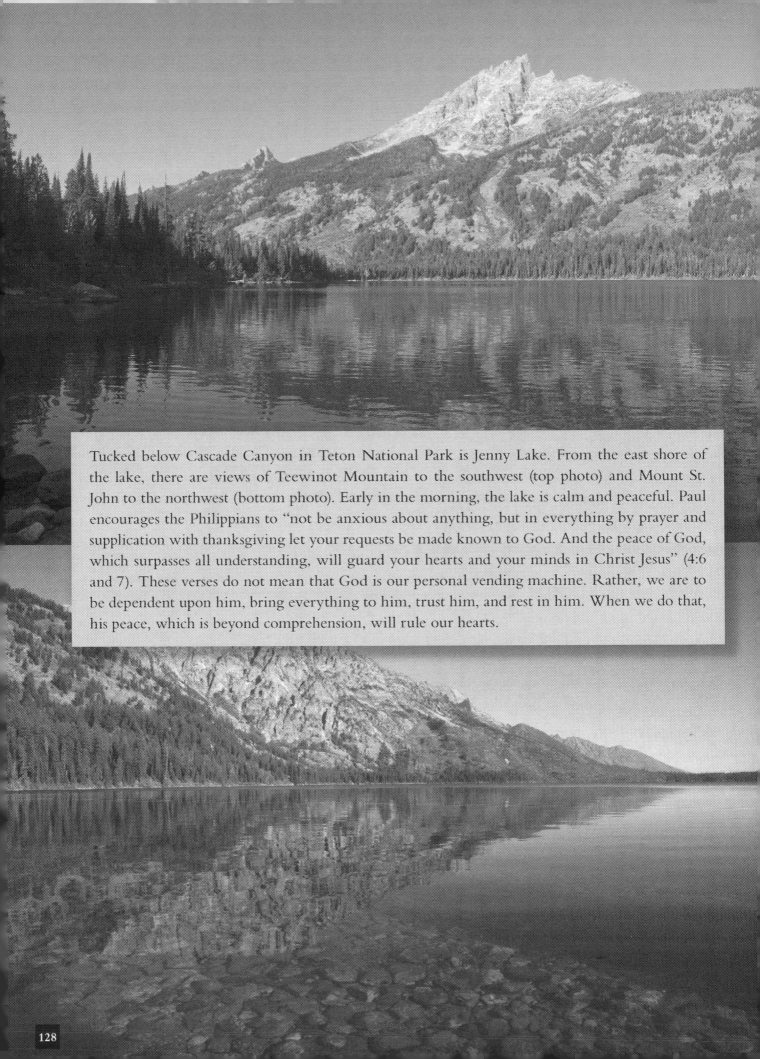

Tucked below Cascade Canyon in Teton National Park is Jenny Lake. From the east shore of the lake, there are views of Teewinot Mountain to the southwest (top photo) and Mount St. John to the northwest (bottom photo). Early in the morning, the lake is calm and peaceful. Paul encourages the Philippians to "not be anxious about anything, but in everything by prayer and supplication with thanksgiving let your requests be made known to God. And the peace of God, which surpasses all understanding, will guard your hearts and your minds in Christ Jesus" (4:6 and 7). These verses do not mean that God is our personal vending machine. Rather, we are to be dependent upon him, bring everything to him, trust him, and rest in him. When we do that, his peace, which is beyond comprehension, will rule our hearts.

The Blue River has its source near Quandary Peak in the Ten Mile Range south of Breckenridge, Colorado. It flows north in and out of Dillon Reservoir (our favorite) and then empties into the Colorado River near Kremmling. Being largely fed from mountain snow melt, the Blue River is a favorite of fly fishers. First Peter 2:5 says, "You yourselves like living stones are being built up as a spiritual house, to be a holy priesthood, to offer spiritual sacrifices acceptable to God through Jesus Christ." This verse refers to the body of Christ (the church) in which we serve one another and worship our awesome God. A house has many different parts, just like the human body has many different parts. Each part is critical to its effective function. Every Christian has been given talents or gifts to use for God's glory. We should remember that any sacrifice or good deed is only acceptable to God as it is given in humble thanks for Jesus's unspeakable gift.

Cascade Canyon is a deep valley in Grand Teton National Park. After climbing above Hidden Falls, the canyon levels out for almost three miles, providing easy access into the mountain backcountry. Teewinot Mountain (on the left) is almost 4,000 feet above the valley floor. The psalmist says, "Bless the Lord, O my soul! O Lord my God, you are very great! You are clothed with splendor and majesty. The mountains rose, the valleys sank down to the place that you appointed for them" (104:1 and 8). He is awesome in power, beauty, and sovereignty.

The Booth Lake Trailhead is just a couple of miles east of Vail, Colorado. The trail rises 3,000 feet over five miles in the Eagles Nest Wilderness and ends at this beautiful alpine lake near the tree line. Hikers are often treated with an appearance from local residents. The aspen trees were in all their glory this crisp, fall day. As the prophet Isaiah said, "How beautiful upon the mountains are the feet of him who brings good news, who publishes peace, who brings good news of happiness, who publishes salvation who says to Zion, 'Your God reigns'" (52:7). There is great news! The wages of sin is death, but the gift of God is eternal life through faith in Jesus Christ. Jesus paid the sin debt that I was utterly helpless to pay. He took my place. Nevertheless, he rose from the grave, victorious over sin and death, and because of his great mercy, I have life.

Fall in Summit County, Colorado is simply beautiful. The aspen trees turn brilliant yellow. The air is cool and crisp. But as the leaves change color and the high elevations receive their first snows, there is a real sense that winter is just around the corner—a season that is cold and harsh (unless you ski). Psalm 1:1–3 says, "Blessed is the man who walks not in the counsel of the wicked, nor stands in the way of sinners, nor sits in the seat of scoffers; but his delight is in the law of the Lord, and on his law he meditates day and night. He is like a tree planted by streams of water that yields its fruit in its season." Do I "delight" in the Word of God? Is it a treasure to me? The fall photographs are a reminder that seasons change. Winter indeed may be coming. Life's situations change. Difficult days may be near. However, for the person who treasures God's Word, there is a firm foundation for he is faithful. In due time—"in its season"—that person will bear fruit for God's glory.

Bibliography

Chisolm, Thomas. "Great Is Thy Faithfulness." Hymnary.org. Accessed August 29, 2022. https://hymnary.org/text/great_is_thy_faithfulness_o_god_my_fathe.

Crosby, Fanny. "He Hideth My Soul." Hymnal.net. Accessed August 22, 2022. https://www.hymnal.net/en/hymn/h/334.

Hemphill, Joel. "He's Still Working on Me." Lyrics.com. Accessed August 29, 2022. https://www.lyrics.com/lyric/7586805/He's+Still+Working+on+Me.

Johnson, Brian, Jeremy Riddle, and Christa Black Gifford. "One Thing Remains." Lyrics.com. Accessed August 29, 2022. https://www.lyrics.com/lyric/22163090/Jesus+Culture/One+Thing+Remains.

Mote, Edward. "My Hope is Built on Nothing Less." Hymnary.org. Accessed August 29, 2022. https://hymnary.org/text/my_hope_is_built_on_nothing_less.

Neal, Antonio, Marshall Hall, and Samuel C. Mizell. "There Is Nothing Greater Than Grace." AZLyrics.com. Accessed August 29, 2022. https://www.azlyrics.com/lyrics/pointofgrace/thereisnothinggreaterthangrace.html.

Ortega, Fernando. "Give Me Jesus." Divine Hymns. Accessed August 29, 2022. https://divinehymns.com/lyrics/give-me-jesus-fernando-ortega-song-lyrics/.

Robinson, Robert. "Come, Thou Fount of Every Blessing."Hymnal.net. Accessed August 29, 2022. https://www.hymnal.net/en/hymn/h/319#1.

Wade, John Francis. "O Come Let Us Adore Him." Hymnary.org. Accessed August 29, 2022. https://hymnary.org/text/o_come_let_us_adore_him.

"A Wonderful Savior" – Fanny Crosby
"There is Nothing Greater Than Grace" – Point of Grace
"Come Thou Fount of Every Blessing" – Robert Robinson
"Solid Rock" – Edward Mote
"Great Is Thy Faithfulness" – Thomas Chisholm